ACCURATE MEASUREMENTS

Adam White

Doire Press

First published in April 2013.

Doire Press
Aille, Inverin
Co. Galway
www.doirepress.com

Cover design & layout: Lisa Frank
Cover image: Diarmuid Russell
Author photo: Karine Perdriel

Printed by Clódóirí CL
Casla, Co. na Gaillimhe

ISBN 978-1-907682-22-3

ACKNOWLEDGEMENTS

Acknowledgements are due to the following publications in which some of the poems in this collection first appeared: *The Stony Thursday Book; Skylight 47; The Shot Glass Journal;* and *Miller's Pond.*

Heartfelt thanks for all the encouragement and the opportunities to read or recite many of the poems in public, to: John Walsh, Lisa Frank, Kevin Higgins, Susan Millar DuMars and Pete Mullineaux.

For her time and careful consideration given to each of the poems, a very special thank you to Karine Perdriel.

CONTENTS

for my mother

Roofing

The first thing you do is check the building for square.
Below, hoary-headed masons, who've never laid
eyes on you, tidy away tools, shove lukewarm
bottles of stout between tight lips
and spy you prizing the dumb harmony
left by the lump hammer, trowel and plumb line,
slung to the bottom of an old tool-box-cum-stool
snapped shut just in time for lunch.

Depending on the weather, deal wall plates
slap or clonk into place. They're butted together,
and what's sticking out's trimmed
by the teeth of a savage oil-spitting chain.
A ridge poll is offered up to the empty heavens.
But lean rafters, like joined hands, are
raised in reverence to Pythagoras,
who was one of us.

Now crackling felt is rolled out, bobbling along a lath.
With a pencil poised on one ear, you make your way
to the apex, careful not to puncture this sealed hold
of silence inside: quiescence to be sold, owned and passed
down to the youngest son.
Take your time as you alight from the lashed ladder,

hit the ground before the evening's first rain;
tomorrow you will do it all again.

Accurate Measurements

No one ever got the hanging of a door right
first time round. That's what makes it beautiful
to go back to time and again.
You can almost grasp who came before you
by how the frame is cast in the mason's
block-on-edge.
Eyeball it for plumb, improper pencil marks,
feel it up for haphazard handsaw cuts;
tell somebody's casual endeavour
from a ceremony where nothing
is accidental.

    You could spend the morning
fiddling with a jack plane, worrying
about taking too much off one side of a door.
In the end it's all in the correct
housing of the hinge, a chisel's whetted lip
and hammer staking out their right of way
clunk by clunk. And flakes of feathered wood fall
to ground, crackle under boot, cavities
puffed clean into which the cool obliging brass
will sit.

    Manhandled into the jambs, it's
a barrier mid rooms of industry and ease.
The master comes checking up on a past pupil,
the thickness of a coin
between your toil and his.

The fitting of the lock's
snug if done squarely. We've moved along
from the quiet elegance of brace and bit
to shooting two hundred and twenty volts
of hot augured steel, whining and thrashing,
into the stile, the stile hocking up lumps
of itself in the rout. But signs of horseplay
are hidden in the finish, and putting on
handles is dainty work.

Hung accurately,
a door doesn't just close: made to measure,
it clicks into place.

Some carpenters
hang their best door in a bathroom, others shine
in toilets, mindful of those who will sit there
later, relieving themselves, taking it all in.

A Bad Fall

Again the long-drawn-out lunch and slightly
overgrown men sitting behind newspapers.
Obviously no place for new blood
to break camp first, he waited (whetting an
appetite on talk of an afternoon's
assignments) for someone else to stand,
eventually released like a dog
from the trap to find no hare out running.

As the drone of engines drowned out thirty
minutes' silence, he regained his morning's
whereabouts, hurrying up steps of pitched
masonry, the best part of the crew still
smoking in the wings, declaring the cunt
of a week's back broken. It was then he met
with the steel, a span of a ton hopping mad
down two gable ends as if in accusation:

had his newcomer hands left the toughened beam
sit out the last half hour in a compromising
position? Next, a cartwheel back to ground
and the one stroke of luck: the steel banged down
before his head. Though for us it was the same
as a boiled egg dropped storeys down to a tiled
floor, he was blessed that the order (steel
then head) had not been the other way round.

Months later he appeared to tell of
the repairs: screws and a plate in the forehead,
pins all down the left of his face. Someone
said 'well you're baptised now' for laughs.

But watching the eyes be prisoners behind
the bars of a surgeon's best efforts, you could
only feel fortunate: it wasn't you
who'd tousled with steel, who'd fallen on it.

This House

Conducting rain to scourge ground sodden and mud-logged,
trailing sheets of it by a house and in off the sea,
at the tail end of November, winter's
suddenly here and furious
for having been forgotten. Now it's taking fury
out on the unborn; all it wants to do is drown
the pale bald head of a day.
So I wake in a gale that's flaking rain
against the unlit glass of my eyes,
that stuffs down my ears a sound, a sound
that's a squall rip-roaring on the high seas,
though when I went to bed I was on land.
By now wind has countersunk my ears to hear nothing
but winter shouting out all other sounds.
On a rattly rigging of iron up
and eight-foot boards across, I try to thaw
into my rounds of a drifting house. Out on deck
alone, I am the lookout who planks a crow's nest
of sorts, and I am the first: already weather
has banged all the angles out of last night.
I fix another plank above my head
to climb higher for a better look about,
to get over slates at eaves that piss down
like a row of taps left on. But every time
I lunge another leg of scaffold skyward,
I see nothing but smouldering horizon's
watery red beaten out by steady downpour,
and rain is pressure-driven down the sleeves
of my oils. Rain has taken on the plastering
of walls and chimneys. With all its wet weight it slams
doors and windows on a house full of men in trades,
drags heavy curtains of its standing gallons past.
I'm frightened to the point of understanding

that we may as well turn round, but know that
being this far out now means capsizal,
and this house is sure to founder:
shipwreck on the homestretch for one,
but the maiden voyage of another.

After Snow

Snow has made headway impossible.
A long night of falling slowly is three-inch-caked
on all yesterday's good work,
so any roof in slate is like a tilted rink
and every horizontal's bearing white.
At the gate vans shelved down with tools wheelspin in
smoky fits, frustrated on frozen rutty ground
by winter's hardest weather yet.
I said as much, backing off the ladder's
bottom rung last night, said a sickened underbelly
of a grey sky threatened such non-cooperation.
On the roof now you'd mistake the makings
of a snowman's head for a beam's hard edge, for sure
footing; a quick slip'd uncouple you
and your work. You'd drop down for bursting
on a poured floor set like pack ice,
soil the concrete's clean sheet as helplessly
as would a big bag of dampened down slack
offloaded from that height —
though in a different colour.

In the bottom of the leathery pouch
on my belt nails gang, lead-heavy and lumpen.
They won't come out but sit there nipping
stung fingers that can't find them individually.
So we're grounded for the day. Staying on
means doing big awkward things down here —
going is to mope at home till dinner.
We'll dismantle planked scaffold, then slow circle
and get up another house in its infancy
for major surgery. We'll pick up wasted half blocks
and wet bags with a fist of hard cement in each:
masons' mess tossed off every finished gable.

We'll clean up after other trades all day.
But there is no shame in that. Shame is recalling
yesterday's roof to cut and the right day
to do it, yet how many times I cursed
what I thought was quitting time and wasn't.
Now this morning everything's in fancy dress
and crunches foreign under foot, everything's
fat in the hand and unmanageable.

Our Promise

Sometimes, in the rush of things, scaffolding,
stood like pairs of roofers' high heels, has
to be quickly stripped, and will be off bringing

out potential in a new house when the time to lay
a ridge and finish the old has come. So like a flag
we hoist an apprentice to where, for a day,

with a wet sponge, he will smooth and stamp
the sand of the company's seal. He'll
necessarily lord it, working out cramps

through unhurried but called-for gymnastics,
knowing one false step means tobogganing
to certain death. Balanced there, he sticks

the crown down as guarantee, rejoins
that 'a roof should last a hundred years', coins
our promise, but is alone at coronation.

In June

Above in bed, I heard the shovel —
or perhaps it was a spade —
slicing soil, some of which my mother made
by carrying those buckets full

of juice-losing peel to the barrel in
the garden:
       my sister stabbing

with belief down into the guts
of the black garden. The order
given: quarry a last place for
a decomposing dog. You must

take to task, be strong on your feet.
Stiff and leaking from his rear end
slowly, he was starting to smell and
they were the nuts and bolts of it.

I cast his last meal to the birds
on the roof of the shed. Fourteen
years calling him laid to rest in
my throat, but still dead set on words

of humour: 'Shall I throw a bone
in with him?' A gaucherie met
by my mother's gaze, and yet
another command: 'Get it done.'

Dead fall shovelled in to conceal
an old friend,
       the soil dead level

when we glumly mulched the grave where
big-heartedly, and for him, in
italics, I should have written:
Dubh — thank you for having been here.

Winter Visit

She will only say the new stove
was delivered and fitted for
a song, that the coalmen prove

novel, labouring on the yard's steps
and cramped path bearing bags, nursing
them overhead and down onto their breasts

to feed the bunker half a ton.
But I only see her lugging
buckets, the skin round her thumbs

react to dust, hear on a cold
morning what the doctor said about
porous hip bones and then behold

my mother stoking up a house.

The Helmsman

Over the stove in my mother's kitchen
hangs *The Helmsman*, replica behind broken
glass, souvenir of more turbulent
times when, saying he felt like change, my father rent

the image from the wall one night. From beneath
the clamp of his thumb, cracks trickled
until someone spoke up, and worse followed:
the print was gummed to the thin sheet

of glass. The rest of us thought it was a shame:
the helmsman in there, chest to the tiller,
guiding the vessel into a port, never
to see our undivided light again.

Though it was always hard to tell if he'd decided
on his steering or manoeuvred the till
half-heartedly, whether he fixed straight ahead
or dreamed of where gulls capered on the littoral.

Now my mother is there alone. Some
nights the stove keeps her warm. Above it the surround
keeps track of our movements. Postcards, come
from where we go away to, all around

that same broken docking scene: what we can't pronounce
wedged between the busy lip and sheet. Mouths
gone far, overseas, send word that the frame
ever gave more governance than the helmsman.

Her and that Wardrobe

At first glance that wardrobe was good for firewood,
for the havoc of a quick hammering
in the yard below and best burned by Christmas.
What had you there but a pair of run-down doors
to hide the old outfits, a bottom so
Swiss-cheesed in woodworm it could hardly
keep a drawer off the floor, a heap
of neglect then against the bedroom wall?

But when taken in hand it was not that.
When rubbed down with a steaming cloth
it started to tell of something else.
A few worm-plundered planks replaced,
dry joints rooted out for squeezing in new glue
and a pair of handles would set it off again.
So you took it outside on a fine day
in August, chisels hard ablaze
and the blade of a saw kept warm all day,
soaked in preserver stray wormholes turned fumaroles.

That evening it was back in its corner,
stinking of a workover, with all
the signs of the years you'd added on.
Or was it those it now claimed back?
Her Saturday readying herself in
its glass, a door open to shuffle through
and choose one dress for two, find the earrings
to go with, swinging to time as if time meant
forever. The drawer always slightly open,
the flash and frill of unmentionables.

And won't you return here in a year
to see the ass fallen from another drawer?

Won't you come back to take out tools
and attempt the impossible,
start speaking from the hands again,
your dumb language wanting to promise everything?

Turbine

for Max

When you've driven all you can take in
of Wittmund for a day,
just ease your foot off the pedal
of the rental car and pull in.
Sand, whisking in the ditches, will
compartmentalise nice light greens
and yellow all the way to
the coast of Lower Saxony
without you. You'll miss no clump of
trees, no relief or vantage point.
But get out and stand under a
wind turbine, let into your arms
the tower standing two hundred
metres out of nothing but sand,
and you're as if suddenly in
on a family secret:
all day here, Max, comes the best of air
to sweet-talk batting blades, to spend
whole nights turning on man's mechanics.
Overhead, the whoops of a
sluggish clock's hands are tick-tocking
life down into and across
the flatlands, even out onto
Langeoog, the *long island*,
your grandfather's fatherland,
lighting up bedroom desks for
homework, heating the evening soups.

Dam

No one here.
 No one need be here.
  This dam, just by sitting, did it all.
   This thirty five-metre-high cast belt of concrete
    stopped a torrent, stonewalled its passing. The river
     stopped running and put on weight. The
      river lay around and turned into a lake. A
       river that used to pitch past and spit in your face
       is now a sheet of still water,
       is assuming everything else's face or tired of
      not doing anything. The dam is
     not pretty on its backside (it's concave, shored up
    for maximum restraint), but turns out enough electricity
   for you and I to leave on twenty five thousand
  televisions all day for a year. Yes, that many
 televisions left on necessitates stopping up a river.

English for the Workplace

I teach English (but English for the workplace) two nights a week:
conversation skills that can't be killed due to such sheer disregard
on the back line, nouns with dry mouths found in the trenches,
biting their fists—vocabulary lists for the desperate. On Tuesday
evenings I school them in asking politely for customers to serve,
shoplifters to observe, for beds to make, someone else's children to
feed, change, cradle and wake, even to earn a living from someone
lording it in the castle of Gort who wants you to walk his mutt,
keep a sharp eye out for fear his pedigree shit might sit in the
wrong place. And for tables to wait on: he who is used to snipping
pieces of furniture from lengths of wood he's had reduced to the
right size, who once hewed a roof out of a tree his father felled.
Mine father carpenter too. He builded lovely house in Kraków. Is
very big.

Wednesday is a workshop for words you need in greeting,
dealing in urbanities, adjectives that brand the self. For this we
pass around the medicine ball of intonation. It's a sweaty gym of
vowels and consonants where pupils like pugilists come to build
up tongue muscle, await the weigh-in for the first round of formal
introductions, unforeseen meetings, even G.P. consultations. It's
a right left, punching the 'S' left unexpressed and no one here
is allowed throw in a damp towel of inarticulation. I pair them
off to pretend across tables that they've never met, to extract
rudimentary information. The classroom becomes a drop-in
centre for recovering mutes: she who composed her thesis on folk
music in Kundera, who translated the meaning of her childhood
into free verse. The carpenter and the scholar—the poet trying to
get a stiff word in edgeways. Mine mother poet also. She publish
in Czech. Is very, very difficult. Everyone say hello.

In Sheffield

A steelworker with a four-storey face
defines a Sheffield street.
He might be sitting for a photograph.

Yellow hard hat, navy blue shirt, collar
concealed by the cream cotton scarf that smartens
him up, it could be his last day on the job.

This is built to not look down on you:
a mural in brick, art framed in a gable,
fifteen thousand muck sandwiches heaped to the rafters

where, composed, he is looking to retire
in 'the ugliest town of the Old World',
race pigeons most days, still stir his tea with pencils

and nails in a shed at the bottom of
the back yard, far enough to not hear grandchildren
worry about being out of work.

Now steel is made and brought from elsewhere.
Metallurgy here has given way
to automation, wages spent fast on

the old sites where men and women laboured,
spent from making them.
He could visit the Metalwork Gallery

in the Winter Garden. A dragon made
of stainless steel forks and spoons welcomes you
at the sliding doors. They'd tell him Sheffield's

knives are mentioned in *The Canterbury Tales*,
show off tea services and turtle
soup tureens in thick glass cases,

though there's not a tempered wood chisel in sight.
They'd sell him a postcard of a steelworker
with a four-storey face that defines a Sheffield street.

When they built those four storeys of expression,
pulleyed different colour bricks up onto
scaffold to lay them, a hand's breadth mattered,

but for some this was just brickwork by numbers,
beginning a new course only meant getting
things done. The art stopped there.

Note how the blue of the shirt was used amply
in one eye, a brick too many bulging
out into what looks something like a tear.

Woman with Two Children at a Sale of Work

parries through bustle of bags bulging out,
purses flushed into biscuit tins and fast cash.
But the initial sense of an extravagance
soon boils down to easy math: costs less to buy clothes here
than stitch and patch what's left in the council house.
She'll dress and shoe the youngest two
with bus fares saved by thumbing 30k,
the others instructed to knock up
the Murphys with sandwiches, knives washed and dried
and sliced pan put back up high.
Her husband's style of casual labour
hounds him out of doors daily bar none,
sometimes morning, mostly after evening meals.
Even when work is slack, or a dead cert
fluffs another race, he won't back down
or stoop to straight answers, but stomps around
pumping up his chances of a job.
And standing drinks against each promise
of a day's work is a day's work in itself.

Woman with two children at a sale of work
spots her youngest naming off cakes with quick eyes.
When finished trawling tables top heavy
with a town's bottom drawers that would no longer close,
she'd like to have him carry home a box
by the crossed twine that keeps it shut
and promise that tonight he'll shout 'cream buns all round',
or something else as festive, after beans
and chips to use up last year's potatoes,
and leave it shut to hell for once,
the ledger of what's practical
and their life's little pleasures.
But she mustn't lose the run of herself,

not while the competition excites, says again
that here it's all for next to nothing,
when for her it's merely less of a strain.

Danny Meagher

Weekend or day of the week, it's nil to him;
a month to liquidize the army invalid pension.
Slows down to Guinness when the wad shrivels to double digits,
come the first he's toasting Midleton Distillers again.
Weather only registers as more or less light
for a shave at the sink, to fry up the breakfast by.
Butters a pan for six strips of bacon,
four rounds of pudding, empties the lot on two cuts of bread,
flushes it down to a cast iron stomach
and sterling pipe work at sixty.
Coffee as black as the river on his night watch in Africa.

Thirty years he's been through the seasons
in a green sleeveless shirt tucked in tidy.
Khaki slacks. Belt buckle shining.
Shoe leather polished back to black and buffed,
regiments the hair he's left with oil and comb
for the impact of rain and gale
in a weather-drummed town on the west coast of Ireland,
where he studies his step to enter a bar.
Sits on his own at the end of the counter;
ignored like the rest of our statuary to history.
Where he stares into, no one has asked him ever.
Steels his gait when he comes off a stool for the bog door
or front door. Drunk as ten men never misses a urinal,
or turns from the bowl till it's spick-and-span.
Never leaves by the back door.

Under a helmet of baby blue, he killed in the Congo.
Self-defence at range so close he checked the temperature
of blood with his tongue, and tasted the salt in the blood
of a warrior shot in the face: a boy wearing nothing
but guns, copper paint and a necklace of diamonds

down to his prick, screeching the lingo
as if a third atom bomb were about to be dropped,
until his head was lopped in a firework burst of bullets.

If his cheeks are alive with coursing balls of single malt,
his eyes are walled up in a glaze
and have had their greedy fill of living.
They're hiding the change that happened inside,
for he sits in a fog of forgetting Katanga,
that his love was the army, but not what's in it,
that he scuffed the paint of peace-keeping
and saw the dollar-green of never-ending trade,
that if his gut is imperturbable,
his heart is lost in a darkness since.

Maam Cross

Driving out to Letterfrack through Maam Cross,
we note hay stacked up five bales high.
I say admirably, but what I wish
to be able to say is why,
and why wellingtoned men would queue
at a caravan's steamy open hatch,
so I pull in. It's for a few
sandwiches it turns out, and tea on tap that must match
night pints for thirst quenching, if any there's the one
that assembled those fair bales so well. On a wall opposite,
others look fed and watered, to have gone
across the road to doff their caps and sit
on a ancient stone in contemplation.
Telling myself that I might learn something, I stroll
over with my one relevant question:
'Is there anywhere we might get petrol?'

Soon there are introductions. 'Forty years
in farming' — one offers — 'hereabouts', then expects
my counter, some acknowledgement.
'We're from Youghal in east Cork' — a sudden fear
it's not enough — 'Once full of factories;
quiet now.' With that tongues loose,
veteran grins come out. The communiqué proves
to be an open sesame.
'Same everywhere. I heard somebody say
the Connemara pony went from five grand
down to two. It wasn't really worth that much and
now the men with concrete on their boots can't pay.'
In the car you ask me why we stopped, seeing
the fuel gauge point up at half full.
I only say that just as much as our words well
picked, words poorly chosen must mean something.

Boys and Their Toys

Now you have marble hearts
and the name of every
boy failed at Letterfrack.

Where there were only slabs fat-faced
with moss, saying nothing,
they've cut in granite's black

the age of each child swept
under the grass but one,
when digging a hole was easier

than being exact:
Walter Footer died
as a young boy, 1910.

A lead soldier breaks from too much bending.
A lead soldier's thrown back
in the pan for melting,

and miniature cars
left in lieu of flowers
mean some, as young as eight,

will never grow up.
Here 1918 was an ugly year:
only weeks between burials,

if disguising evidence
in Christian rigmarole
could be called burial.

At one end of the mass grave
a stone cross in white
is still standing. At the other

a stout pillar holds the gate
where someone had the bright
idea of setting

an Irish five pence piece,
stuck it tails up
in the drying cement.

So somewhere
between the stone of that cross
and the harp's mettle lies

our imperishable
history beneath toys —
the cut and dried story of all those boys.

Innocence Overheard

'Two girls and I would pick wild garlic
and go there to play a game:
the first to find a date of birth
on the stone hearts the same

as, or closest to, that day's date,
should lie on the ground,
before the heart, their green
and white and cry that birthday found.

Until of course we heard they were dates
on which each boy died,
and feeling there was something that had lied,
we played something else.'

An Awakening

I

Last night on the island. Brendan
waving a knife, dishing out bloody
pollock over a slow game of chess. Barely
out of the waves, he had them in the pan.

I set bait to have the queen reeled in,
but was checked by the advance of morning,

the rising tide come to ferry us
out of unfinished business.

II

'Just in time', the thickset skipper
teased through his watertightened beard,
and lubberly we reeled onto rolling boards,
launched bags down from Boffin's New Pier.

As the vessel made knots, ploughed graceful lines through
the dull might of trough and crest,
the group spread out absently — abaft,
starboard and some towards the bow —

but I stood there like a seeking
compass, lost to your constant tacking.

Nearing Cleggan someone came out of the bridge,
our safe debarkation laid to his charge.

'Islands are great places to
meet people', he said, gesturing back
across the Sound, offered me a pocket map
of the island where I had just met you.

Travelling Back

You may say that too many miles
separate A from Z for you to squeeze
us closer on the bedside globe, or
even hold the distance between thumb and finger.

Turning leaves of a found school atlas
reminds with old authority that one
can't be in two places at once,
and an intercontinental ocean

that you might get your lips around
sunders us really, on a scale of one
is to forty-two million.

But on this side geography's no obstacle.
I've a map in mind allows free travel
the breadth and length of you, have found

the page that reverses cold ratio.
Remembering the fathoms of a hot bath
I have you (lines of the hands lat-
itude), encompassing waist line to land and chart up your

long back's falling waters. I'm a mad staggering pirate
returned at the shoulders' ledge: vista of the other side's landlocked
soft hills, and all again my *terra percognita*.
Close both eyes at the head to breathe, beneath a

canopy of forestry feel rivers defining cool,
revising my geography of you.

A Fall in the Snow

One evening,
the air about me whispering,
the flurried snow
fine-smoking over country roads,
I walked into a forest and cheered how
heavy fall would cancel my only bearing homewards.
But the forest was stripped to what winter had done to it,
a jacket of white was stifling the life from it
(a weeping willow had frozen to a helmet of frost),
and still your last words to me repeating into it,
and the angry, living sob that mine to you had cost.

Then, was it a hidden branch or rock
that stopped my advance, steady and tank-like,
or some idea the right thing
to do was name solutions, and not a guilty
party? I remember nothing but crumpling
on the snow-swollen floor of the forestry,
getting up to feel the great wide world
between us of no importance now,
and finding another way back to the house, where snow
was coming down off the eaves like downward
smoke, to say these words
to you.

Dawn Light

When the lamp that hangs above the table
hangs again in the window pane
and floods light on the very same
desk and pencil, the window in the gable

is a mirror backed with blackest night
for backing. Everything you know, or need,
or that proves credible for the time being, is stored
aboard, within reach of where you write

from. But as sure as the sea sinks a ship's
punctured hold, soon the room's a hold that's slowly stoved
by daylight; your desk's a bridge that slips
from its long night's vantage point. The lamp has moved.

Now suspended from the shape of a tree,
now sitting on the roof of the dark block of a shed,
the light in which you're losing interest quickly
starts to soften against the day, consumes its own edge.

The world renewed happens in the garden.
The lamp smudges to suggestion while plants harden
around it. Your eyes tire from looking on
a work of portrayal for too long.

Switched off, the lamp's a lighthouse veiled in the sun's brilliance,
finally worthless in the lack of any sense of absence.
And the room is just a place to hide;
you unbolt the door and go outside.

The Squirrel

late September, hasn't time
for school kids' rowdy nature observations,
or tired hikers sipping tea,
their Great Outdoors scrutiny and search
for sense in breaking in new boots,
new resolutions.

For even the quietest
of woodland walkers, only the sudden
overhead rustle, leaf jostle, or one too-quick-
dipping limb, or smudge of russet in the thicket —
gone is the squirrel, busy keeping pace
with the sun's every disappearance

and altered appearance,
each slight change in the temperature of woodland,
where nature is doing its utmost
to spoil her plans to put on weight for winter,
to fatten her pelt
for a bid at a litter.

The tops of trees
are filling out with ways to gestation
(for now both promised bountifully
and guarded in a very hard shell),
but every nut's
beyond its obstacle:

this branch is a forest
erupting from the side of a tree;
this one's a dead end
(exacts the perfect long jump
and balanced runway landing —
sure-fire aerial

                acrobatics only
across the breach in leafy green),
                and every third's a hurried climb
                or incline, with nothing but claws barely
going into bark and a low belly to win
at cheating gravity.

                Gravity that commands
the forest turn its back on the sun,
                that drives the first yellowing leaf
                groundward, flag-starts a stockpiling race
to the general fruitlessness
of deepest winter.

                The brain she was given's
the size, shape and implement
                of a walnut, for puzzling a fuzzy
                map of her ration-packed crannies'
camouflaged whereabouts. Not finding dinner
will be a constant source of stress

                (though her nose
for the rubbed-on scent she left will prove
                its worth ten times before memory
                delivers a single nut), and the crow
never forgets a place. His sneak-silent eye
hangs cloaked

                in a black hole of himself,
studying dig and concealment to the end.
                Only when the squirrel has scampered back
                to an honest day's work will he snigger
food and freeloadery to his feathers,
unmask his beak

long enough for
a good root in the forest's freshest cache.
        Beaten by others to the look and animalising
        smell of corpulence, no squirrel mate
will give her chase along the naked boughs of trees
through winter's rock bottom,

        when all four seasons
come closing down to this: if a lone crow
        can thieve one nut from her,
        then a murder of crows can murder
a litter before she's even had
the chance of carrying it.

Tying the Knots

If you're close enough to a man's lips
to watch him wet the woven gut ends,
to see the surgeon's knot he's made close in,
summoned spittle stop the line chaffing on the line
(friction'd only make a pig's tail of it)
and the hook bopping against the back of the hand,
you'll get a first taste for fly fishing.

Looked at this way
the hook is literally dressed to kill
in feathers from a former hunt,
when the rifle
dipped lower than the fishing rod
and levelled out
and banged big game all over dry land.

But it's the eyes invite you to appreciate
what he's done with spare time:
pimped hooks' slender steel up to the nines.
The shanks wear their boar's hair real tight
round a hard body,
look good enough
to just picture a fat trout sipping down
its titbit, its quiver slapping off
to cut up current.

He promises you the bite and barb of
these pretty little things
will do the real damage though.
They'll break into the cold-blooded palate
when artful slack straightens into a stiff yank.
They'll steal in and be caught rotten
behind the river-ramming scales.

Learning to Cast

As with instruments in brass,
where getting the breathing right precedes
any catch of correct notes in the sky,
so your hours of hands-on lessons
in the fishing rod's unpunctual physics
and aping Maelzel's metronome
will all come long before anything
you'd call conjuring up a salmon's diet.

Because knowledge never happened by accident.

You'll spend all your fishless mornings
in an open field ignoring nearby rivers.
Sunsets peppered with midges will go by
conducting nature music until
you're sick of it before you have dry flies
get down to imitating real insects,
before whipping the air that hangs
over water vanishing past into
a believable feast and backing out
with your deceived dinner on a long leash.

Catch the Trout of Your Dreams

'You can come here, spend the day fishing
on a card. A loyalty card means
every eleventh day's free of charge.
And I'll keep numbers down to ten or less,
guarantee a certain peacefulness,
a strict minimum of freedom to fish.'
The light leaving Mayenne country,
he was pressed to show all he'd invested
weekends in, preparing for the fall
of a calendar page, the licked-wet thumb
that sets it off, the season's starting gun.
              'The men who own this land
have no interest in the river that keeps one
off the other. Him this side only says
it means relationships stay cool, ever
running smooth, and he'd leave it so,
but I pay for privilege and say best
make use of an asset. All I want's rights
to a path, to slash a good metre wide left
and right and I'll have clients out here come
April with this in mind: to catch the trout
of your dreams, to hold mother nature
in your bare hands — at least they owe me that.'
Something then said he hadn't finished. 'Though
I released twenty kilo further down
last month, and ten of carp, a fish farmer's
finest at five euro a kilo,
and can't find them now. As a rule I get
one bite in a dozen casts. Usually
round this time at every other look there's
a jump or a smack at the surface.
But now nothing', and he toe-poked a stone.
The stone rolled into a plop, then plumbed the deep,

as it might a dead fish he'd spied and swept
back under the river, the river going cold
black while a shiver shook the breadth of it.
    'Now there's plenty parking up here. I've had
it scraped flat and gravelled, so you can get
what gear's needed ready at your ease
and try your luck this side, then go over
further down in a small boat. I got that cheap,
tied ropes across so you can draw yourself
back and forth. It's satisfactory.
You might get your ass wet crossing, but a bridge
my brother proposed would mean sinking more
money into the thing. And safety
regulations mind, more time spent — you have
to think of all that.'
                It was one unsure foot
after another following him up
the bank, out a fresh gap through briars rent
back to bare stalks, standing to attention
in the dark. Then a big sign, car-length,
head-height, all of a sudden flashlight-lit:
"Domaine des Rêves" — trout and carp.
No kill – hooks without barb
or barb filed down only. 10€
per day. For card call Jim (no more
than 10 cards on any 1 day)
06 41 89 34 09.

Crime Scene

Fish, drying out in death, dusty
mouth agape like the mouth
of a disused mine.
And just as the stink catches
on your last breath
there's enough of them to topple a wheelbarrow,
scattered out as bricks go in a gangfight,
dry enough for stacking.

Eyes that flashed once into the heart
of the Atlantic and back, muscle that pulsed
underneath a running film of fatty oil,
look like old discoloured coins now
and carcass, conked
out but two foot from a sup of river.

Big Brown Trout

Deep-living, unseen,
some brown trout can feed for years and pile on
thirty pounds, sleep long like a four-foot log:
unbothered geographers
on the bottom of a lake.
       To fish them is another kind of fishing.
       Where a slip of river trips and tumbles
over boulders it's rushing,
even old men are sure-footed, stay upstanding,
       see flashes of a scaly back
       just when a taut line means today's first catch,
and won't risk a thorough soaking
by taking on a trout on a trout's terms,
       only work backwards to the nearest bank,
       satisfied by guaranteeing
each new foothold,
or relocating, reusing old ones.

But trolling from a boat is like sitting on skin
stretched over the belly of an underworld.
To trawl the bottom with bait you wait.

You have to believe the granddaddy
of them all is still alive,
       down there
patrolling his underwater fields,
slipping past cliffs of lost cities, a solemn thing,
displacing scree with submarine energy,
bottom feeding at a pace like slow murder.
It's a fish only as big as the part
you have in the history of fishing.

Hooking him in the side of his mouth
is like snagging anchor
on the open door of a car.
          That deep,
he'll play you back and forth for hours,
suddenly unforgetting deep-seated wildness,
testing what you've learned to trust of fish
and tackle with his tug and change
of direction for heavy ammunition,
trying you for limits you've learned to live with
until he's reduced the fruit of your first
thrill to a single stone of wisdom.

If rolled into a boat, a fish like this
is never eaten. Stuffed still, glass-cased
and finally believable,
it's hung on a pub's wall for storytelling
beside its brother caught a century before,
proof of a world
and feats of the old ways staying deep,
living in who needs to bring it up.

Gull and Cormorant

Life isn't always as it reads in the evening
where the tide builds to high tide.
The sea's feasting on a croissant of sand,
then gasping for it again,

and untroubled gulls can compass perfect circles,
easily survey beach for bread crusts and rind
so low they're a wing beat from clipping land,
or coast air back up high enough when a gull's-

eye view is better of their hunting ground.
But the cormorant's constantly scrapping the hunt,
a rummager resurfacing with a haven't-yet-found-
that-fish-I-got-a-flash-then-a-glint-

of look. Returning to working the size
of his fishing and flying gear bottomwards,
he swims nearly half a mile in two dives,
and all the underlying effort's lost in human words:

he's checked the same water more than once,
frantic unorganised search party of one,
might *frighten* up his food, black head banging round
like a loose signpost that gives you nothing to go on.

Still, enough to catch the reconnoitring eagle-
eyed gull, trigger its quickness into cant,
its over-practised hurled-dart dash down a cleft
in the rising air. And for every hit that's cancelled

at a metre a further's called: one bird
airlifted wide of the field as another's
blitz-stiffened wingspan hatchets the water,
its fish-packed bill's bull's-eye looting in the tide.

Vietnamese Pig, Parc Saint-Nicolas

It even swills its sleep,
this snoring wreck of a pig, pot-bellied
out in a hollow. Can't get enough air;
has to snort through all those folds of fat.
Can't get enough sleep;
every greedy snore is a whole-faced fart
dragged up a snout that's squashed at the
wall of the pit by the weight of its owner's pig bulk.
Swatting off flies with a bristly ear
to defend each easy second of slumber,
it's as if it had put away a sack
of feed that should have done a week before
slouching over here and slumping into sleep.
Swine, packed plump in the hide
that's sun-dried grey and dusty black where it isn't
caked with the muck of the dugout.

So the girth of this mesh fenced-in pig
is nothing like the cut of an abandoned
animal. No end, lobbed-over contraband
is never only sniffed at;
this spayed sow makes up for offspringlessness
through gluttony, gobbles the ham from every
school lunch sandwich flung in fascination.
If having no cure for hunger, always
looking for it anyhow, is being a real pig,
munching meat to the vision of a pig
on a spit with a mouth red apple-wedged open
and roasting, has to be cannibalism.
But the most, and the least,
she can show for it is a distended gut.
When times are tough, the price of nearly
fifteen years of pig fodder no longer

fits the family picture. But this one's lucky
(civil servant of a showroom pigsty),
though oblivious to luck:
its overlapping lard hammocks down
over the eyes, a binge-dangerous
accumulation of brimming troughs
and rotting cabbage heaped.

The Paul King Players

written to the instrumental 'Change Your Mind'

Fat, pitched, steel strung from head to body
pulsing at belly level, the bass has gone all
out, pummelling the back straight of a song.

It's getting a rubdown mid race. Then
another bend at this late meeting; the
trumpet's bearing in, but on its last breath,

followed by the drum's well-timed dedumph firing
when asked, breathing down the trumpet's brass.
All to play for when the King takes the lead,

prising open the pack with a little
wristwork. Every rocking body's in place
for the whips to crack out, instrumental

on the last stretch of track. Neck and neck
now, the close group is careering fast,
and you stand too, feel the volume come up,

put down your pint glass to embrace a blanket
finish. But as the entourage flattens out,
the dark horse of a bass is still in it,

bumming out quick feet, pauses rather than stops,
follows that up with a flick and a twang,
stumbles over the base line again.

The Flutist from Savoie

What is it he breathes into that pipe held
level? Eyes shut to us, but the shoulders
dip and reel, has our curiosity
up, out of its basket like a charmed snake.
Amidst the pub's low hullabaloo, all
concentration, as if one blunt note would
burst the bubble he's a-whistle into.
Pursed lips flatten bellowed air flowing hard
across the first hole, and not a whisper lost
in getting there.
        Yet the tune seems to carry
him from the present.
Is the flutist searching Savoie, finding
his way, finding home then best with eyes closed?
Huffing and puffing, rib cage shifting gears, stealing
up endless steps of notes and swapping jigs
with sails of wind to spare, he'll blow this house
down well past closing time, before he's
finished will have us neither here nor there.

New Year's Day

It's New Year's Day and you and I must cut
this timber stove-length. To get all logs stacked
neck-high in a wall, we have until
such time as want of light denies a car
off home sufficient time to see a tree
stretched across a bad bend on a country road.
In the storm just passed no one saw the shattering
oak when the hinge broke in the falling mast,
no one heard the crack echo far away,
or the drop pulp surface mud and pound frozen ground.
But the gravity of a tree,
that neither you nor I could get two arms
around, blocking the way that links neighbours
in a modern sense, on a day as short
as this, is felt, when it's felt in the gut.
A week or so the far side of solstice
I wouldn't put this right without your help.
We could just saw the lengths according
to where the eye falls and the saw follows
(a length looking two foot something to you
seeming nearer three of my wood to me).
We'd chuck it in a heap that said no more
than public danger quick-averted.
But no, I'll start this year as I intend to end it:
by not returning to old tasks half-done
when fresh ones claim attention easier.
And when the time comes tonight to mark off
your share, I'd rather we walk out your cut
of a clean pile quickly than have to agree
on such terms as guess and estimation.
All afternoon we will saw, barrow and stack
and put up a wallpaper of year rings
off to one side. Then I'll pay in kind

with half a cord of wood I might have felled
(and paid for help) as early as the summer.
Not near as much as you'll have cleared from the road,
but won't you prize my oak through two long months at least
some winters round? And if we do it well enough,
for miles about no one will know, or even
mention, how close they came to a hard end.

Chainsaw

Perfect putt-putting, grumbling idle
between knockdown rounds, the Husqvarna
has lived up to a neighbour's laudation: 'Spend
on a saw as savage as that and you'll not go
short logging any of the woods in the county'.

So let her glugglug good juice until
the trigger's pulled and she farts out loud of
sluggishness. Let her glut precision parts
with hot sawdust and her own oil dribbling.
Isn't cleaning after binges the least

that I can do? True to those words, not once
did she hum or haw, but always, like snarling
watchdogs set upon intruders' bare legs,
no tree here stands a chance. A mob of teeth
chisels that go from some to hundreds

in a hundredth of a second can be
sent to rip a trunk's insides out for
a sniff of petrol. And from every tug
that wakes her, sputtering and maddened,
to the cold hours on the bench under

rag and rasp, she lives out reckless lives
of her own. Now the face cut's done, the saw swallowing
and spitting its chain, legs locked strut-fast
in an upturned V, I'll steer that riot of steel
into the back of another tree.

Estwing

Nothing like the timber-handled,
D.I.Y., do-the-trick variety,
whose head would loosen from pulling a nail,
then need a second hammer to beat a wedge
between the pared handle-end
and the socket in a stubby head
(to remain of some use to you),
that couldn't pull small nails on tidy jobs
because of how wide the claws were spread.

A token, from you, on a day
of qualification, for a promise
to serve my time, kept, four years to the day,
this hammer's shiny shaft and head
were poured all in one go, smelted
from smoking guns down into the handle.
The gap between these claws closed into a hold
so tight you might use it to pull a pin.
Aeronautical head, edged steel shaft
that could stand in for an axe and split wood
for kindling. *Estwing* branded in yellow
on the coal-blue, sure-grip handle,
anti-slip for wet days and accuracy,
for working on heights.

                American hardware.
Over there houses stood in timber
inside and out. A carpenter
got so many hours he could earn as much
as a doctor — with a tool like this.

Next day, on site, let fall,
it clinks back into the holder on the belt

with a fine ringing note, a jingle like
spurs on a boot that turns from a killing
at high-noon on Main Street.
Like reholstering hot iron,
having dropped the last Wanted in the Wild West.

Strike!

Be careful how you start and strike a nail;
if it stands shallow in the wood's grain
the shock of an inaccurate hammer
could leave it on its back, frolicking down off a roof.
And to land, but not land dead square despite intent,
to not lend a brave pinch that might keep it there
whatever the outcome of course metals meeting,
is like to propel it out left or right or head on,
severing air with a snipping sound.
Then you're a nail less and this changes everything.

Admittedly some heads are known to be difficult.
You've bitty brads for the boards of a floor,
others are shaped oval like sailors' caps
and hard to catch because of that.
Tales of ill fortune after a hammer's
smashing out sparks first touch even led men to trust they had
it in them to brand a house as bound to burn down.
Doubtless such talk'd set a wee tremble
in your hold on things when staring down a target.
You'd just as soon give it a playful tap
or two, go on trusting superstition
before your own science.

But I've seen some nails four inches long
pounded in in an act, wire heads kicked in
as if a horse's shoe had done the job,
wood blunt-thump bruised with the brunt
of an anvil-heavy hammer's head
in a blow and peppered rust to mark the spot.
I know that sort of thing's uncommon,
the fruit of a life perfecting the gesture.

So what begins as handling a means to an end
becomes shaking the hand of an age-old friend.

Graduand

for Tom and Mick Fitzgerald

Constant building makes an architect of the mason
                                         — Turkish proverb

From the ground up this house was teaching me.
In the beginning there was a shovel:
a work-dulled hand-me-down missing half its handle,
for banking eight of sand and sixteen gravel
in the back of the mixer. A bag of cement,
jabbed-split, fumbles past the spinning lip last.
And shovelling sand is not the same
as shovelling gravel; the man on gravel
shovels and strains twice as hard. Concrete sloshes
itself into itself, the brimming drum
lists from all this throwing its weight around:
a tilt-turning vat of muck brought up over
our boots from Monday all the way to Saturday
sometimes. But you soon see where you fit in
and put the mess to rights, smack down
and drag along the straightest timber's edge,
turn a lumpy field into a sheet of glass.
Now, for as long as some mother
and father's pilgrimage-back-and-forth
of the small hours may go on, our floor,
set but four inches-thick, will serve its purpose
between the four great walls of their purchase.

Death of another Island

Three islanders from Inishark, 12 miles off the west coast of Connemara, have been missing since they left Inishbofin in a currach at about 5 o'clock last Sunday.

— The Irish Times, *Thursday April 21ˢᵗ, 1949*

Survivors relieved to sit into fishing smacks.
An island of hundreds whittled to twenty three
by the price you pay for insularity.
      Today, with the sea's rare permission
to leave, and fine, but raw, weather for it,
a fishing and farming community
will come out of Shark island.
Pulling the last pieces from a house
(a bedstead lashed across one man's stooping back,
a green kitchen dresser mournfully
shouldered seaward by four more),
it is as if you had to kill it to leave it,
break up dwellings to rule out any return
to such a place of origin as this.
      Here string-tied suitcases
fill a galvanised bath, there hens protest
in gunny sacks and bitter-black
iron pots tumble dully on board a boat:
tabernacles of mackerel and potatoes
they say, hot dinners begrudged
from rosaries fed through desperate fingers,
whitewashed spades slid into soil much like
unpleasant begging letters.
      Islanders, up early
to leave on the high tide an island
forever, as were the three disciplined
oarsmen on Easter Sunday 1949,

whose families are still here now,
though not for long. Some of the most skilled hands
on the Irish coast debarked at Trá Gheal
to gallop for mass in Saint Colman's
after one Lent-long promise (not a dram
for forty days) and all fascination.
Some say they swallowed their fill, sang softly
on Boffin; no one will deny they couldn't
call the tune when Shark's pull meant another
rough crossing. All lives lost
to the belching Sound of the Atlantic.

Islands are expelled yet spelt out
by the hammering sea.
        'Beautiful to look at,
but that'll hardly feed you', I then hear
one old man remark, as salty surf bursts
on the prow of our bolting currach,
leaving the heartache of a limited
and angular land behind, while nature
nudges its cliff-top cemetery into
the yawning sea. 'We'd no youth,
no muscle left to turn a sod,
to haul up the boats', he continues.
'So in this skinning wind we make our way
to the mainland', says another, somewhat younger,
from the opposite side of the boat,
who, it turned out, was his brother. 'And for what?'
'To work', replies the old man.
'To live, Michael', corrects his wife, beside him.
Whereupon the younger asks them both:
'And look away west every morning is it,
from the soil a future's grafted onto,
to where nature reconquers everything?'

Adam White is from Youghal, in east Cork. He worked for many years as a carpenter/joiner before developing an interest in teaching. At present he works in a secondary school in France. *Accurate Measurements*, his debut collection, grew out of a poem that he wrote for the North Beach Poetry Nights' slam in the Crane Bar, in April 2009. The poems that followed were written in Galway, Cork, Angers in France and most recently rural Normandy.